FIVE STEPS TO
EFFECTIVE STUDENT
LEADERSHIP

About the 5 Steps Series

The books in the 5 Steps Series are useful for anyone seeking bridge-building solutions to current issues. The 5 Steps series presents positive approaches for engaging with the problems that open up gaps and divisions in family, school, church, and society. Each volume presents five short chapters (or "steps") on a single topic. Each chapter includes a relevant "excerpt", "insights" from the author(s), and an "example" to consider. The "example" is a real-life story that illustrates how each step can be applied in daily life.

Topics include:

- Facing Suffering
- Living Christian Unity
- Effective Student Leadership
- Towards Great Parenting
- A Fulfilling Marriage

FIVE STEPS TO EFFECTIVE STUDENT LEADERSHIP

Insights and Examples

Dennis Carr,
Michael James,
and Hannah Trost

NCP

New City Press
of the Focolare
Hyde Park, New York

Published in the United States by New City Press
202 Comforter Blvd., Hyde Park, NY 12538
www.newcitypress.com
©2014 Dennis Carr, Michael James, and Hannah Trost

Cover design by Leandro de Leon
Book design by Steven Cordiviola

Scriptural references are taken from the *New Revised Standard Version
Bible*, copyright 1989, Division of Christian Education of the National
Council of the Churches of Christ in the United States of America.

"Principles of Good Practice for Student Affairs at Catholic Colleges and
Universities" are taken from Principles of Good Practice for Student
Affairs at Catholic Colleges and Universities, Second Edition with
Diagnostic Queries (Chicago: Association of Catholic Colleges and
Universities, Association for Student Affairs at Catholic Colleges and
Universities, Jesuit Association of Student Personnel Administrators,
2009).

Library of Congress Cataloging-in-Publication Data

Carr, Dennis.
  5 steps to effective student leadership : insights and examples /
Dennis Carr, Michael James and Hannah Trost.
    p. cm.
  Summary: "Rooting their work in Ignatian Spirituality, Catholic
Social Teaching, student affairs best practices, and a 21st century
understanding of a spirituality of communion, these authors offer a
proven resource for the formation of student leaders"-- Provided by
publisher.
  ISBN 978-1-56548-509-9 (alk. paper)
1. Catholic universities and colleges--United States. 2. Student affairs
services--United States. I. Title. II. Title: Five steps to effective student
leadership.
  LC501.C283 2014
  378'.07120973--dc23
                              2014005961

Contents

Step 4

Step 5

Introduction

HE TASK OF BECOMING human is a lifelong project. We are not born complete. Education at every level must be devoted to contributing something meaningful to this task of becoming fully human. Catholic education is informed by a tradition whose wisdom asserts that the education of the person is the education of the *whole* person. Ideally, Catholic educators, students, and their collaborators accept the responsibilities of fostering genuine community, of creating environments that demand cooperation and mutual support, of providing opportunities for all the members of the community to be served and in turn serving those in need, and of teaching the process of critical reflection on the prevailing cultural values that potentially enhance or damage the human condition.

Student leaders have a particularly rich set of opportunities to grow and discover their own capacity to become fully human — fully themselves. This book offers a five-step approach to developing student leadership practices informed by a spirituality of communion and rooted in a deeper understanding of each participant's moral identity. In campus settings too often marked by isolation, fragmentation, discontinuity, competition and individualism, we suggest that student leaders who practice the "Art of Loving" and live a spirituality of communion will generate counter-currents of interdependence, relational action, dialogue, and reciprocity.

The Ground Floor to the Five Steps

For someone who tries to live a spirituality of communion, the goal of "teaching the individual" really becomes one of "teaching individuals how to recognize God-Love within themselves." In other words, it is essential to begin from the premise that we "Love the Other as Ourselves." Ignatian spirituality calls this concept "reverence." The complementary principle is, as the fifth of the *Principles of Good Practice for Student Affairs at Catholic Colleges and Universities* states, to "challenge students to high standards of personal behavior and responsibility through the formation of character and virtues." These are the conceptual principles at the ground-floor from which the five steps ascend in each chapter capacity to become fully human—fully themselves. This book offers a five-step approach to developing student leadership practices informed by a spirituality of communion and rooted in a deeper understanding of each participant's moral identity. In campus settings too often marked by isolation, fragmentation, discontinuity, competition and individualism, we suggest that student leaders who practice the "Art of Loving" and live a spirituality of communion will generate counter-currents of interdependence, relational action, dialogue, and reciprocity.

The Ground Floor to the Five Steps

For someone who tries to live a spirituality of communion, the goal of "teaching the individual" really becomes one of "teaching individuals how to recognize God-Love within themselves." In other words, it is essential to begin from the premise that we "Love the Other as Ourselves." Ignatian spirituality calls this concept "reverence." The complementary principle is, as the fifth of the *Principles of Good Practice for Student Affairs at Catholic Colleges and Universities* states, to "challenge students to high standards of personal behavior and responsibility through the formation of character and virtues." These are the conceptual principles at the ground-floor from which the five steps ascend in each chapter of this book. And the twin goal of "building the community" becomes, to a certain extent, both the method and the consequence of individuals who are discovering God-Love. The choices of individuals in response to their community (i.e., the relationships that come about) will either damage the community or build it. And the identity of those individuals becomes defined by these choices.

Taking the Five Steps

This student leadership development guide is made up of five chapters, each corresponding to an aspect of the "Art of Loving." The "Art of Loving" is born from an ethos of reciprocal human interaction such as in the Golden Rule. Practitioners have developed a helpful tool called the Cube of Love. Each side of a six-sided die is labeled with a component of the "Art of Loving:"

- Love the other as yourself
- Love everyone
- Share the other's joy or hurt
- Love your enemy
- Be the first to love
- Love one another

At a given moment, often at the beginning of the school day or at the beginning of a meeting, the group will roll the Cube and take the result as their watchword. At another moment, often at the end of the day or the end of an event, students and faculty or supervisors share their experiences of living that particular aspect of the "Art of Loving" throughout the day. Using the Cube of Love has helped schools, office environments, athletic teams, residence halls, and student leader organizations to establish a consistent ethos, transforming their cultures from ones based on rules to ones based on relationships. This changed way of being translates not only into interpersonal relationships, but also into extracurricular activities, student development programming, and academic performance.

Within each chapter or "Step," readers will find:

- **A point** from the "Art of Loving" followed by a concept from Ignatian spirituality

- **A compelling case** for practicing these concepts in daily life enlightened by scripture, Church documents, and student development research

- **Concrete suggestions** for putting the concept into practice. Suggestions are informed by scripture, church teaching, and one of the *Principles for Good Practice for Student Affairs at Catholic Colleges and Universities*

- **An inventory** for personal reflection on how each of us can begin to implement the practice on a deeper level
- **A "real-life story"** from students about how they have tried to put the concept into practice
- **A checklist** of actions that you might take to move towards the concepts suggested in the chapter

Step 1

Love One Another:
Men and Women for Others

Be the First to Love:
Creative Companionship

Love Your Enemy:
Cura Personalis

Share the Other's Joy or Hurt:
Be Attentive

Love Everyone:
Finding God in All Things

Love the Other as Yourself: *Reverence*

The Point

IMAGINE FOR A MOMENT that you are making your way to class and you see a student texting and walking. Completely engrossed in his or her phone screen, the student is oblivious to anything beyond that tunnel vision — other people, the sky, the weather, and surroundings. Suppose that battery dies. Instantly the student's vision expands beyond what had just been easiest and most immediately interesting to take in all those people and things that were previously being ignored.

This broadening of perception from tunnel vision to a more panoramic view of the periphery is the first step in the "Art of Loving." Once you have begun to practice loving the other as yourself (reverence), the next step is to love everyone. This is also expressed in the Ignatian ideal to *"find God in all things."*

"The Sheep and the Goats"

"Lord, when was it that we saw you hungry and gave you food, or thirsty and gave you something to drink? And when was it that we saw you a stranger and welcomed you, or naked and gave you clothing? And when was it that we saw you sick or in prison and visited you?" And the king will answer them, "Truly I tell you, just as you did it to one of the least of these who are members of my family, you did it to me."

(Mt 25:37b-40)

Why Do We "Love Everyone?"

Before we can meditate on how to practice "love everyone," we must tackle the question, "Why do we love everyone?" And the answer to that question is really simple. Because *everyone* is made in the image of God!

The Case

"Creation Story"

> Then God said, "Let us make humankind in our image, according to our likeness; and let them have dominion over the fish of the sea, and over the birds of the air, and over the cattle, and over all the wild animals of the earth, and over every creeping thing that creeps upon the earth." So God created humankind in his image, in the image of God he created them; male and female he created them.
>
> (Gn 1:26-27)

God made humankind with a special dignity not bestowed on any other living thing, and that dignity was being made in His image. This can speak to us in two important ways.

1. **Being made in the image of God means our worth and value are inherent.**

And by inherent, we mean that it is "existing" in someone or something permanently. Often, we value ourselves and others based on data in our resumes, GPAs, number of clubs joined or Facebook friends. Can you think of any others?

15

The one string uniting all of these criteria is that they are *external* to us, and often result from *what we do.*

To practice the "Art of Loving," we must think differently. Our dignity and value is not external, but *inherent*; not dependent on what we do, but *who we are: made in the image of God (Imago Dei).*

Within an educational setting, we love everyone not by appreciating what they can do for us, who they can connect us to, what reference they can give, but *by loving them for who they are.*

2. **Since we are made in the image of God, in God we find how we are called to live most authentically.**

If God is in essence a community of self-giving love between Father, Son, and Holy Spirit *and* we are made in the image of God, *then* we live most authentically when we live in communities of self-giving love.

> The Lord Jesus, when He prayed to the Father, "that all may be one ... as we are one" (Jn 17:21-22) opened up vistas closed to human reason, for He implied a *certain likeness between the union of the divine Persons, and the unity of God's sons [and daughters] in truth and charity* [emphasis added]. This likeness reveals that man, who is the only creature on earth which God willed for itself, cannot fully find himself except through a sincere gift of himself.
>
> *Pastoral Constitution on the Church in the Modern World: Gaudium et Spes* [Joy And Hope], sec. 2

How Do We "Love Everyone?"

A Principle of Good Practice for
Student Affairs at Catholic Colleges
and Universities:

Welcomes all students into a vibrant campus community that celebrates God's love for all.

Student affairs professionals at Catholic colleges and universities are committed to creating inclusive, welcoming campus environments in which members celebrate the diversity of all in both faith and culture. Their works, actions, and programs reflect respect, justice, collaboration, and dialogue.

17

"The Good Samaritan"

(A scholar of the law) who wished to justify himself, said to Jesus, "And who is my neighbor?" Jesus replied, "A man was going down from Jerusalem to Jericho, and fell into the hands of robbers, who stripped him, beat him, and went away, leaving him half dead. Now by chance a priest was going down that road; and when he saw him, he passed by on the other side. So likewise a Levite, when he came to the place and saw him, passed by on the other side. But a Samaritan while traveling came near him; and when he saw him, he was moved with pity. He went to him and bandaged his wounds, having poured oil and wine on them. Then he put him on his own animal, brought him to an inn, and took care of him. The next day he took out two denarii, gave them to the innkeeper, and said, 'Take care of him; and when I come back, I will repay you whatever more you spend.' Which of these three, do you think, was a neighbor to the man who fell into the hands of the robbers?" He said, "The one who showed him mercy." Jesus said to him, "Go and do likewise."

(Lk 10:29–37)

How Can *I* Love Everyone?

In a time and place where you can reflect in silence, ask yourself these questions:

Take Inventory

- Who is in my "tunnel vision?" Who do I already find it easy to love?

- Do I believe that my dignity, being made in the image of God, is inherent?

- Do I tie my self-perception to external factors?

- What external factors mean more to me than they should?

- Who are people I normally consider "outsiders?" How can I be like the Good Samaritan toward them?

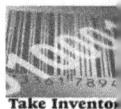

Real-Life Story
No matter how busy you are

KATIE: As student leaders, we frequently find our-selves running from class to class, meeting to meeting, and spending the "down time" in between crouched over our laptops and books in the library. In the pursuit of our fullest selves, it is sometimes easy to forget to share our love with each other. When we are this busy, how can we share this internal light with the people around us?

A wise man once advised the world to "stop and smell the roses." Including others in the aura of your internal light, no matter how busy you are, is not impos-sible. Each day, take a moment to reach out to a friend, colleague, or stranger and share with them your love. While there are myriad ways of doing so, my favorite is by means of conversation.

Do not underestimate the power of conversation. Even brief dialogue and thoughtfulness can transform someone's outlook on his or her day. In my college dining hall, for instance, I always take a minute or two to chat with the cashiers, even if I am grabbing a soda and rushing off to class. I venture beyond the safe conversation of "How are you," "Good, fine, thanks," and ask them about their weekend or if they have had a chance to enjoy the sunshine. Through the accu-mulation of these short but meaningful encounters, I have become acquainted with a wonderful woman named Marie. Although I only see Marie for a couple minutes a week, she always calls me by my first name and asks how my classes have been or if my asthma is getting any better. When I approach the counter, her face becomes alive. It lights up with the kind of love that you can share with others through just an ounce of genuine thoughtfulness.

Similarly, the other day I stopped on my way to class to chat with a janitor who was mopping the stairs in my residence hall. After a couple of minutes of small talk about our hockey team, I thanked him for his hard work and assured him that everyone in my building appreciates what he does for us. He thanked me, and never stopped smiling. His sheer joy warmed me from the inside out, and made being a couple minutes late to class one hundred percent worth it.

Conversations are key to spreading the love that you find within yourself. Whether you mentor an underclassman, help a friend through a difficult time, or strike up a conversation with a stranger in the elevator, you are spreading your love to the world. How you choose to include others in your light is up to you, but do not forget the importance of dialogue. It can be simple and brief, but even thirty seconds of thoughtfulness can leave a lasting impression on others. Take the time to smell the roses, and you will find the light inside of you and that of the world growing brighter and brighter.

- What was Katie's favorite way of practicing "love everyone?"

- What are the most meaningful conversations you've had? How can you use conversation as a way to "love everyone?"

"Love Everyone"

Checklist

❑ See everyone as an ally, colleague, or partner in the education mission.

❑ Make a conscious effort for "transparency."

❑ Give priority to communication. Keep all "stakeholders" in the loop.

❑ Say hi to someone to whom you normally might not.

❑ Invite other groups on campus to collaborate on programming.

❑ _____

❑ _____

(Add any actions you might think of, too!)

Step 2

Love One Another:
Men and Women for Others

Be the First to Love:
Creative Companionship

Love Your Enemy:
Cura Personalis

Share the Other's Joy
or Hurt: *Be Attentive*

Love Everyone:
Finding God in All Things

Love the Other as Yourself: *Reverence*

The Point

ONCE WE HAVE OPENED our eyes and expanded our viewpoint to see the other person, we allow ourselves the opportunity to step out of our own worlds and into theirs. If we are to enter fully into that life of the other, though, we must be intentional in our efforts to pay attention to their experiences and to what might be going on beneath the surface.

Simple daily interactions are a great place to start; they often have much greater impact than we realize. Think of a time in the last week when you could have engaged in a meaningful conversation with a peer or coworker but felt you were too busy to talk for more than a few minutes. Did you ask how their weekend was and go on with your day? Did either of you gain anything from that conversation?

Often our own worries, responsibilities, and issues prevent us from knowing and understanding our neighbors; they keep us from entering into relationships that we think can't be fit into our already-packed lives or that we are scared to enter into in the first place. For example, the awkwardness of sitting next to a peer on a bus and trying to spark up conversation can feel agonizing. The practice of being attentive demands a level of discomfort that most of us would prefer to avoid, but we cannot give priority to what is happening in the life of the other if we are not paying attention.

Why Do We Share the Other's Joy or Hurt?

Being attentive gives us the opportunity to recognize and understand the perspective of the other, thus allowing us to get outside of ourselves and walk in their shoes. Walking in another's **The Case** shoes involves letting go of our own strong beliefs, opinions, and ideas and making the other's perspective our own. This is difficult, and can make us vulnerable as we try to let go of our worries, failures, or imperfections. So why do this? Is it reasonable to expect that we can really incorporate this practice into our daily lives?

In the Spiritual Exercises, St. Ignatius offers some insight into why, as believers, we want to—and can—live out this attribute. As beings made in God's image, we strive to be more like our Creator. And when we are presented with the option to take a more divine perspective and actually choose that path, we become more alike and build our relationship with the one in whose image we have been made. Because God's son became one of us to share our joys

and sufferings, we are being more like Jesus when we do the same.

How Do We Share
the Other's Joy or Hurt?

As involved students, how do we model an inclusive style of leadership that creates communities rather than individualistic advancement? As we compete against our peers for internships, coveted leadership positions, and institutional resources, do we understand their needs, goals, and desires? Or are we only concerned with our own personal goals?

A Principle of Good Practice for
Student Affairs at Catholic Colleges
and Universities:

Creates opportunities for students to experience, reflect upon, and act from a commitment to justice, mercy, and compassion, and in light of Catholic social teaching to develop respect and responsibility for all, especially those most in need

Because the framework of the Catholic social tradition is vital to the work of student affairs professionals in Catholic institutions, it is important for these professionals to become familiar with the tradition and to incorporate it into learning opportunities for students. Central to this work is deepening students' awareness of local, national, and international injustice and grounding this understanding through creative partnering with diverse, underserved communities. Ample opportunities for action and reflection will help all to grow, individually and collectively, in their knowledge and practice of this rich tradition, thereby contributing to the

"At the Home of Martha and Mary"

Now as they went on their way, he entered a certain village, where a woman named Martha welcomed him into her home. She had a sister named Mary, who sat at the Lord's feet and listened to what he was saying. But Martha was distracted by her many tasks; so she came to him and asked, "Lord, do you not care that my sister has left me to do all the work by myself? Tell her then to help me." But the Lord answered her, "Martha, Martha, you are worried and distracted by many things; there is need of only one thing. Mary has chosen the better part, which will not be taken away from her."

(Lk 10: 38-42)

common good and building a more humane and just world.

How Can *I* Share the Other's Joy or Hurt?

In a time and place where you can reflect in silence, ask yourself these questions:

Take Inventory

- What struggle do I most need to overcome, or what might I need to let go of to allow myself to pay better attention to the needs and concerns of those around me?

- Where do I see God at work in my relationships with others?

- How do I let others share in my joy or hurt?

Real-Life Story

Stopping to ask a real question

KATIE: I started thinking about the shallowness of my passing conversations while at a BC dining hall.

"Hi!"

"Hey! How are you!?"

"Good, you?"

These little snippets are not disingenuous, just impatient. There isn't even enough time in the small time (within sight and earshot) for the second person to respond! And because I walk places so fast, I end up tootling around on my phone or remaking to-do lists when I could have stopped to ask the acquaintance a real question. I thought of at least five people that I've waved to for four years without ever stopping. Though understandable — we can't be close to everyone — it's a shame. Though Boston College has a reputation for being a friendly school, I couldn't help but realize how superficial some of these friendships are.

After this moment of self-reflection in the sandwich line, I turned around to find my roommate chatting with someone she knew from a summer service trip. Her lunch date, Paige, had lived on my hall — directly across — sophomore year, but we'd never exchanged more than a few words. Both trying to be polite, we started talking about shallow things. I mean, it was sad that the summer was over, and it had been quite hot the past few days, but I could have this conversation with a librarian or a new neighbor! I'd known this girl for two years! I decided to use this opportunity to delve deeper.

I knew (thanks to Facebook) that she'd been abroad for a whole year, studying in two different places. Once I'd asked her a few questions about that and shared that I, too, had just been abroad, we started talking about the strange transition we'd just been through. Returning from another country, where it's possible to be relatively anonymous and more independent takes a lot of adjustment. She started talking about her changing group of friends, and her reverse "culture-shock." We'd each been changed by our experiences in so many ways; we knew it would be difficult to come back to our "old life." It was amazing how easy it became to talk as real friends.

This conversation has helped me continue trying to share the other's joy around BC's campus. I've found out that there are few benefits to rushing through life, especially while at college. I've always admired others' willingness to care, and now I have begun to discover how easy it is to be that person.

- How did Katie enter into the life of another that day? Why might this have been difficult for Katie to do?

- Can you think of an example of a "superficial" relationship in your life? How does that relationship play out in the day-to-day? Have there been opportunities to share in their joy or hurt?

"Share the Other's Joy or Hurt"

❑ Try to look at arguments from all perspectives and all angles.

Checklist

❑ Put myself in another's shoes before making judgments about them.

❑ Pay attention to feelings that arise when talking to a friend about a problem they're having, or about an accomplishment they've had.

❑ Make an effort to go beyond the "culture of nice." Try to have a genuine, authentic conversation today.

❑ _____

❑ _____

(Add any actions you might think of, too!)

_____

_____

_____

_____

_____

_____

_____

_____

_____

Step 3

Love One Another:
Men and Women for Others

Be the First to Love:
Creative Companionship

Love Your Enemy:
Cura Personalis

Share the Other's Joy or Hurt:
Be Attentive

Love Everyone:
Finding God in All Things

Love the Other as Yourself: *Reverence*

The Point

IMAGINE FOR A MOMENT that you are on a ship at sea, and you find someone adrift in a lifeboat. If your ship passes close, it will be very easy to help — you will only have to let the survivor climb aboard. If the lifeboat is far away and can barely be seen, however, you will need to change your course. It will require more time and effort to maneuver close enough to rescue the survivor.

This extension of help, even to someone who is not close to us, is the next step in the "Art of Loving." Once you have begun to practice sharing the other's joy or hurt, the next step is extending this practice even to those for whom we initially feel little or no empathy or love: those we perceive as enemies. To do this, the Ignatian ideal of *cura personalis* or "care for the whole person" is helpful. It will be explained in the suggestion on page 36.

Why Do We Love Our Enemies?

Before we can meditate on how to practice "love your enemy," we must address the question, "Why do we love our enemies?" And the answer is really simple. Because Jesus, in His preaching, said to not be content with showing love only to those whom we find it easy to love! From Mt 5:43-48 Jesus states matters fairly clearly:

The Case

> "You have heard that it was said, 'You shall love your neighbor and hate your enemy.' But I say to you, Love your enemies and pray for those who persecute you, so that you may be children of your Father in heaven; for he makes his sun rise on the evil and on the good, and sends rain on the righteous and on the unrighteous. For if you love those who love you, what reward do you have? Do not even the tax collectors do the same? And if you greet only your brothers and sisters, what more are you doing than others? Do not even the Gentiles do the same? Be perfect, therefore, as your heavenly Father is perfect.

How Do We Love Our Enemies?

We can begin to "love our enemy" by suspending our pre-judgments and assumptions. To illustrate this, it is helpful to extend the shipwreck analogy from the opening of this chapter. Consider the scenario where the shipwrecked person is close to the ship already. In that instance, we see the person up close and accurately. Now consider the second scenario where the shipwrecked person is farther away. In that case, the literal distance will coincide with a mental distance—between what we imagine the person might look or be like and what is the person's true appearance and personality. As long as there is distance, there will always be that discrepancy. To love our enemies, then, we must close that gap, *suspend our pre-judgments and assumptions about the person.*

In college, we encounter students, faculty, and others from a variety of unfamiliar geographical locations, cultures, upbringings, and viewpoints . We must consider that our "enemies"—those we find annoying or otherwise disagreeable—have been formed differently than we have, and so react to situations differently.

Cura personalis is the Ignatian ideal of attending to the care and development of the "whole" person.

Creatively look for **graces already present** in the person or situation.

Creatively look for **graces that are possible** in your relationship with this person.

These two ways to "love our enemies" involve *cura personalis*. Loving our enemies requires us to resist the temptation to focus upon and magnify in others what annoys, disappoints, or repels us about their actions or personality. Succumbing to that temptation reduces others to a two-dimensional caricature of their true and authentic selves. Therefore, with a humble sense that not everything about us is fully agreeable to those we encounter, we must creatively look for graces *already present* or *possible* in others — regarding our would-be "enemy" as a whole, multi-dimensional person: *cura personalis*.

Sometimes we perceive someone as an enemy because of a particular incident in our relationship. Another key to loving our enemy is forgiveness. Hate only begets hate. Only forgiveness can break the cycle. Hate continues to harm, but forgiveness absorbs a past wrong for the sake of love and a new beginning. And our Teacher was the first to show us how, even at the hands of those who were crucifying him...

"Forgiveness"

Two others also, who were criminals, were led away to be put to death with him. When they came to the place that is called The Skull, they crucified Jesus there with the criminals, one on his right and one on his left. Then Jesus said, "Father, forgive them; for they do not know what they are doing." And they cast lots to divide his clothing.

(Lk 23:32-34)

Student affairs professionals who work in the Catholic tradition and serve in institutions of higher learning have a twofold call: to articulate a compelling truth as we understand it and to search for an informed truth as we explore it. While the first is supported by the rich heritage and reflection of a faith community, the second entails openness to other traditions and experiences. Educational institutions thrive on dialogue respectful of differences of points of

Principle of Good Practice for Student Affairs at Catholic Colleges and Universities:

Seeks dialogue among religious traditions and with contemporary culture to clarify beliefs and to foster mutual understanding in the midst of tensions and ambiguities

view, and the consequent uncertainties and tensions are vital to the learning mission of colleges and universities. Thus student affairs professionals serving in Catholic colleges and universities honor other faith traditions and experiences and invite them into dialogue for purposes of exploration and insight.

How Can I Love My Enemy?

In a time and place where you can reflect in silence, ask yourself these questions.

Take Inventory

- Who I have I cut out of my life? Who have I walled off from myself?

- Am I willing to work a little more to close the distance between myself and someone I perceive as an enemy?

- Which perceptions of my "enemy" are true and which are assumptions that I have made or find it easier to believe than the truth?

- How can I build on graces or strengths already present in my "enemy?"

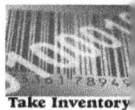

Real-Life Story
A Gift

MARIA: It was 9:00 p.m. on a Wednesday night in February, only two short weeks before Boston College's housing lottery was scheduled to begin. I was walking back to my Residence Hall after an hour-long meeting, carrying 72 pages of reading still hot from the printer. Although I was upset with myself for not starting my history homework earlier, I was fairly confident that I could have all three articles read by 12:30 a.m. Just as I was approaching my residence hall, however, my cellphone rang, potentially shattering all hope of getting to bed at a reasonable hour. It was my friend Olivia[*] calling from a study room in O'Neill Library. From the shakiness of her voice, I could tell she had been crying. "What's the matter?" I asked, nervously awaiting an explanation.

Olivia told me that she had been in the library, shut off in that study room, for almost an hour. One of her roommates, Katharine—the one she had felt closest to, in fact—had just told Olivia that none of her current roommates wanted to live with her the following year. I believe the words Katherine used were "too nice." Olivia was *"too nice"* to live with them, whatever that meant. Through frustrated words and barely audible sniffles, Olivia asked me to come to the library

---

[*] Names in this story have been changed.

and talk with her. She didn't have anywhere else to go. The last thing Olivia wanted was for people to see her crying, and she certainly wasn't going back to her room to face five girls who had just stabbed her in the back.

I had a choice to make. Either I could tell Olivia I had too much homework to do and promise to see her first thing tomorrow, ensuring I would get some much needed sleep, or I could head back to the building I had just left and be present for a friend in need. Someone once told me that there are two ways to see another person: as a gift or as a threat. Though Olivia was one of my closest friends, in this moment I unquestionably viewed her as a threat. I knew that if I were to go talk with her, I would be there for at least two hours. Either my homework or my sleep would suffer, for I would not be able to do both well if I returned to my room at 11:00 p.m. not having started my history readings.

As I was making up my mind, I recalled the ideal of "Love Your Enemy," and remembered hearing about the positive effects of embracing difficulties as golden opportunities. Now was as good a time as any to practice the attribute of courage. I decided to see Olivia as a gift, not a threat, and embraced this challenge as a chance to strengthen our friendship. I will never forget the gratitude evident on Olivia's face when I walked into that study room with gummy bears and Oreos, ready and willing to listen. Even though I had to finish my reading in the hallway outside my bedroom door and did not get to sleep until 3:00 a.m., I knew I had made the right choice.

- How did Maria perceive Olivia at first as a threat? Why didn't she regret changing her mind?

- Who or what life situations do you perceive as threats? How might you view these as gifts or opportunities?

"Love Your Enemy"

❑ Embrace difficulties and challenges as golden opportunities.

❑ Recognize your adversaries as a gift, **Checklist** providing special relationships and insights.

❑ Be ready to "start over."

❑ Practice active listening *and* listening first, before speaking.

❑ Eliminate "enemy" from your vocabulary.

❑ Embrace difficulties and challenges as golden opportunities.

❑ _____

❑ _____

(Add any actions you might think of, too!)

_____

_____

_____

_____

_____

_____

_____

_____

Steps

Step 4

Love One Another
Men and Women for Others

Be the First to Love:
Creative Companionship

Love Your Enemy:
Cura Personalis

Share the Other's Joy or Hurt:
Be Attentive

Love Everyone:
Finding God in All Things

Love the Other as Yourself: *Reverence*

The Point

*A*FTER BUILDING UP THE courage to love our ene-mies, we must act on that courage to truly live like Christ and strengthen our relationship with God. This requires using that courage to take the first step—being the first to reach out, the first to start a conversation, the first to love.

Most of us find being the first to love terri-fying and risky. It requires an unfamiliar way of being social, a different equation for social interaction. It is easy to enter into a relation-ship with and show love to those who have given the go-ahead to interact with them. We generally have no problem showing love to a roommate, a family member, or a teammate. But what about everyone else? It's uncertain how others, especially strangers or people we don't know well, will accept our kindness and our love. We cannot wait for someone else to open the door. We must open it first.

Why Are We the First to Love?

Ignatian spirituality calls us to look for God in every part of our life—every day, every action, and every personal encounter. We often seek God's call in our vocation. What must I do to fulfill his will—to serve him and his creation? Who is he calling me to be? Similarly, the "Art of Loving" asks us to turn to God, to be attentive to how he is present in our lives and in our daily interactions with others, to ask, *"What is the will of God in this moment, with this person?"* The answer is simple: to love that person. We are called to love. Through that love, we most fully experience the love of God.

The Case

We are constantly being filled with God's grace, God's love. But we are also called to respond to that grace and build on it by sharing it with others. Even though our pride or insecurities might make this difficult, we will become more capable of giving and receiving that grace if we practice the "Art of Loving."

Living in Community

But if by this social life the human person is greatly aided in responding to his destiny, even in its religious dimensions, it cannot be denied that men are often diverted from doing good and spurred toward and by the social circumstances in which they live and are immersed from their birth. To be sure the disturbances which so frequently occur in the social order result in part from the natural tensions of economic, political and social forms. But at a deeper level they flow from man's pride and selfishness, which contaminate even the social sphere. When the structure of affairs is flawed by the consequences of sin, man, already born with a bent toward evil, finds there new inducements to sin, which cannot be overcome without strenuous efforts and the assistance of grace.

Pastoral Constitution on the Church in the Modern World: Gaudium et Spes [Joy And Hope], sec. 25.

How Can We Be the First to Love?

How do we take initiative, to be the first to say a kind word or do a good deed? The first step is recognizing that everyone is worthy of your love. Whether it is a stranger or someone who has treated you poorly, each deserves your love because like you, they are made in the image of God.

It is also important to be the first to respond positively. While in a meeting or working on a group project for example, responding negatively can stifle the group's creativity and energy. But being attentive to the good intentions of those around us allows us to share constructive ideas and resources, thus using the best ideas and talents in the room for the success of the entire group.

Finally, when practicing being the first to love, we must also pay attention to those courageous folks who are the first to love us. When another reaches out, we must be willing to accept that love. This can be hard to do, and it is also easy to miss if we have made prior assumptions about others' intentions.

Principles of Good Practice for
Student Affairs at Catholic Colleges
and Universities:

Invites and accompanies students into the life of the Catholic Church through prayer, liturgy, sacraments and spiritual direction

Catholic colleges and universities assist all students to develop an active and meaningful relationship with God. This is accomplished through such activities as traditional and contemporary prayer opportunities, small faith sharing groups, retreats, spiritual direction, and (upon request) RCIA [Rite of Christian Initiation for Adults] instruction. In addition, liturgical and sacramental opportunities are scheduled on a regular basis for Catholic students. Each student's personal relationship with God can be further deepened by application of the charisms and spiritual practices of the institution's founding religious order, where applicable.

In many Catholic institutions the campus ministry staff is part of the student affairs division. In other Catholic institutions student affairs professionals collaborate with members of the campus ministry staff. In welcoming students to the salvific richness of Jesus Christ, student affairs professionals have a responsibility to understand and articulate the Catholic faith and to support and work with campus ministers to provide pastoral care and leadership to students seeking spiritual growth.

How Can *I* Be The First To Love?

In a time and place where you can reflect in silence, ask yourself these questions.

- How has my own self-doubt crippled my ability to love?

- What can I do to slow down so that I recognize the opportunities God gives me to step out and be the first to show love?

- When has someone shown love to me? How did it make me feel?

- How does being the first to love strengthen our relationship with God?

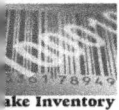

ake Inventory

Real-Life Story
Men and women
for and with others

KENNY: After an incredible birthday week-end in New York City, I boarded a bus back to Boston College. I got lucky with an awesome seat on the bus at a table with some very comfortable legroom. There were still three vacant seats around the table and our bus was relatively empty as we departed. About two hours into the trip we got word that another bus from the same company had broken down on its way to Boston from Washington, DC and that ours was going to take on some of its passengers. A mother, a third-grade boy, and his twenty-year-old brother from Tennessee all sat at the table with me. I decided to take my headphones out and start a conversation with them. I quickly learned that while I just had one of the best weekends of my life, they were having the worst. They left Tennessee at six that morning and had already been traveling for close to eighteen hours when they boarded my bus. Their bus from Washington, DC was stuck on the side of the road for two hours and the family already missed their 10:15 p.m. connection from Boston's South Station to their final destination Bangor, Maine. They got lucky and were able to schedule an 11:15 p.m. bus from South Station to Maine, which would still be another four-hour trip. This however was all before the mother said to me that none of them had eaten since they left Tennessee at 6:00 a.m.

I talked with them throughout the two hours we had left until we reached Boston. While I had been dreading just traveling from New York City for four hours I realized that this family was going through something I could not imagine. I learned that they were going to a family reunion to meet the mother's new nephew and to visit her father's grave. I played card game after card game with the two boys and shared some great laughs along the way. I told them about all of the sights in Boston and a little bit of my story as a student at Boston College and growing up in New England. Those two hours flew by in no time. We arrived at South Station and the family had to rush right to their next bus. Getting off, I was not ready to say good-bye yet because I was so full of their love but at the same time I had so much empathy for their situation. These people had gone twenty hours without a single bite of food. So I decided I needed to put my love into action and help this family during the worst day of their summer. I got off and immediately ran to McDonald's around the corner in the terminal. I bought four number 2 meals with four Sprites, one for me and three for them. It was 11:12 p.m. when I got the food and I chaotically sprinted down the middle of South Station and finally found them still in line just about to board. When they saw me coming they all looked very confused but when I handed the mother the food, she was in shock. A tear ran from her eye and the boys' eyes widened like it was Christmas morning. It was pure joy on their faces. I will never forget that look as long as I live.

The mother all of a sudden realized she did not yet know my name. She asked me and after I told her she thanked me, gave me a big hug, and I wished them farewell. As I walked away the boy yelled back to me with his southern hospitality, "God bless you!" It was right then that I knew God was present. He put me on that bus to help that family. I was meant to be sitting at that table where nobody chose to sit at first. Boston College's motto, "Men and women for and with others" rang in my heart so powerfully that night that I left South Station and boarded the T back to BC with the biggest smile I have ever had on my face.

It was on the train back that I decided to check Facebook on my phone and I suddenly had a new friend request. It was the mother. She had remembered my name. I immediately accepted the request and this time a small tear fell from my eye. I was the first to love but she was attentive and loved me right back. She and her family left Maine later that week and she posted a status: "Leave Maine tonight and heading to D.C. This was a wonderfully relaxing trip that brought me lots of laughter, tears, and new memories. God has been so good to me." I read that one morning when I woke up and again was reminded of how God is ever present in the world. The most honest thing I have ever known is that God is love and his love is everlasting because he works through people. I was the first to love not by being a hero or saving a life, but by simply buying a hungry family some food.

- How was Kenny the first to love? Did this take courage?

- What apprehensions might Kenny have had on his trip that would have kept him from loving these strangers?

"Be the First to Love"

- ☐ Remember that everyone is worthy of love.
- ☐ Challenge the status quo for social interaction on campus.
- ☐ Make the effort to understand the other's perspective before making assumptions about their intentions.
- ☐ Look for moments today where God is calling you to love.
- ☐ _____
- ☐ _____

(Add any actions you might think of, too!)

_____

_____

_____

_____

_____

_____

_____

_____

_____

Steps

Step 5

Love One Another:
Men and Women for Others

Be the First to Love:
Creative Companionship

Love Your Enemy:
Cura Personalis

Share the Other's Joy or Hurt:
Be Attentive

Love Everyone:
Finding God in All Things

Love the Other as Yourself: *Reverence*

The Point

*I*MAGINE FOR A MOMENT that you are a professional musician, a violinist perhaps. You have the score for an orchestral arrangement, and you are seated alone onstage in a full concert hall. Surely when you play the part for the violin, you will play it well. And for one violinist, it could not possibly sound any better or fuller. However, within the larger context of an orchestra, with the expertise of other musicians, their scores, and their instruments, there is a possibility of something more, and something fuller—*but it cannot be realized alone. It can only be realized with others.*

Such collaboration is the next step in the "Art of Loving." Once you have begun to practice being the first to love, the next step is collaboration, being able to "harmonize" our gifts and personalities with the gifts, talents, needs, and personalities of others in a spirit of reciprocity.

Why Do We Love One Another?

The Case

The answer to that question is really simple: We love one another because we are *called to love as Jesus loved us.* John 13:34-25 makes it clear:

I give you a new commandment, that you love one another. Just as I have loved you,

you also should love one another. By this everyone will know that you are my disciples, if you have love for one another."

In fact, the roots of the "Art of Loving" can be traced to Chiara Lubich, a teacher in Italy who, during World War II, came to embrace a certain passage in the Bible. We also love one another because we are *called to be united as one human family as God is united within the Trinity.*

"Unity, Chiara Lubich, and Focolare"

As they took refuge from the bombings in a dark cellar, they opened the gospel and read by candlelight the solemn page of Jesus' prayer before dying: "I ask not only on behalf of these, but also on behalf of those who will believe in me through their word, that they may all be one. As you, Father, are in me and I am in you, may they also be in us, so that the world may believe that you have sent me" (Jn 17:20–21).... As Lubich remembered, *"One thing was clear in our hearts: what God wanted for us was unity. We live for the sole aim of being one with him, one with each other, and one with everyone. This marvelous vocation linked us to heaven and immersed us in the one human family. What purpose in life could be greater?"* [emphasis added] (*Essential Writings* 17).

Michael James et al., *Education's Highest Aim* (Hyde Park NY: New City Press, 2010), 35.

How Do We Love One Another?

We love one another by being more aware of our own gifts and potential, as well as those of others. The onus does not lie entirely on us to do everything ourselves, although the pace of contemporary society and collegiate life may make it seem like we are living in a jungle where everyone has to fend for himself or herself. Instead, by loving one another, appealing to others' gifts when we need help or stepping up when others need us, we help build community and collaboration that enables us to do much more together than any of us ever could have done alone.

The Ignatian ideal of "men and women for others" is key to our understanding of *how* we love one another. We are not men and women in isolation, but men and women interconnected, interdependent, and in community. To become "men and women for others" involves:

- being *attentive* to those around us, those we readily see and those we do not, as well as to those in need and their needs, and to the ways in which we are all connected;

- being *reflective* about others' needs, our abilities, others' talents, and our own;

- being *active* by translating our reflection into reality, "harmonizing" our gifts and talents with the diverse gifts and talents of others to work towards answering the calls of those in need in our society... in other words, being *contemplatives in action*!

Principle of Good Practice for Student Affairs at Catholic Colleges and Universities:

Enriches student integration of faith and reason through the provision of co-curricular learning opportunities

The Catholic tradition has always valued and engaged in dialogue about the interconnection and integration of faith and reason. This dialogue and integration is a legitimate and significant part of Catholic higher education. Catholic colleges and universities foster the development of the whole person. In addition to rigorous intellectual development, there is particular emphasis on a student's faith and spiritual development. In collaboration with academic colleagues, student affairs professionals provide educational opportunities and learning experiences outside the classroom that complement learning in the classroom, such as living-learning residential communities, volunteer service activities, and service-learning opportunities. Catholic colleges and universities provide opportunities for students to develop a habit of reflection and to value prayer in bringing both faith and reason to the discernment process of how to live out their learning experiences and the values of Catholic higher education in their personal and professional lives. Catholic colleges and universities also provide opportunities for intellectually informed and robust conversations on important issues of faith and culture, including applying relevant Catholic teaching to these issues.

"Golden Apple"

The golden apple of selfhood, thrown among the false gods, became an apple of discord because they scrambled for it. They did not know the first rule of the holy game, which is that every player must by all means touch the ball and then immediately pass it on. To be found with it in your hands is a fault: to cling to it, death. But when it flies to and fro among the players too swift for eye to follow and the great master Himself leads the revelry, giving Himself eternally to His creatures in the generation, and back to Himself in the sacrifice, of the Word, then indeed the eternal dance "makes heaven drowsy with the harmony."

C.S. Lewis, The Problem of Pain
(New York: Harper Collins, 1940), 158

How Can I Practice
"Loving One Another?"

In a time and place where you can reflect silently, ask yourself these questions.

Take Inventory

- What are my gifts and talents? Where are my weaknesses?

- How can I "harmonize" my gifts with gifts of other people in my dorm? Class? Clubs?

- What are the pressing needs on my campus? Where are the opportunities for unity?

- When in the past have I practiced reciprocity? Where have I seen good examples of collaboration?

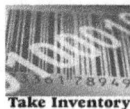

Real-Life Story

Being in community
with those around you

TEDDY: On a Thursday in early Spring, I had meaningful experiences of mutual love at my daily meals. Paying for my egg sandwich and orange juice at the dining hall, I began to talk with Ada, the cashier, about each of our families and how we each celebrate the Easter season. We both laughed about how our families eat so much on Easter brunch. We then high-fived before I went off to my first class.

My dinner was shared with a few little boys who were at a temporary psychological and behavioral unit where I volunteer. For an hour I had them explain to me how to play different card games and the rules of football, even though I knew everything that they were telling me. However, they took such pride in sharing what they knew with me, that I kept pretending that I had no idea.

None of these conversations may seem like anything out of the ordinary, but they really do define what it means to be in community with those around you. I was very different than the people with whom I shared these moments. We had different ages, races, sexes, faiths, socioeconomic backgrounds, and jobs. However, each one was vitally important for my day. "Being men and women for others" does not have to mean starting a non-profit or donating all of your clothes to the poor. It can be seen as being men and women *with* others. The high five, the intent listening, and the courteous curiosity were all examples of just being there for someone else in my life. Striving to give the best version of myself to others every day is not only very fulfilling, but it benefits each and every person I come in contact with. And in this giving of myself I gain the gifts of receiving insights about an appreciation for and the necessity of the other in my life.

- How did Teddy practice "love one another?" Does practicing "love one another" always involve large and grand deeds?

"Love One Another"

Checklist

- ☐ Commit yourself to the good of your constituents, colleagues, and community.

- ☐ Share our hopes, ideas, needs, time, and gifts.

- ☐ Accept what others offer as if it were your own

- ☐ Be attentive to the gifts and needs of others.

- ☐ Build community by practicing and sharing the six attributes of the "Art of Loving."

- ☐ _____

- ☐ _____

(Add any actions you might think of, too!)

_____

_____

_____

_____

_____

_____

Appendix

Student Leadership and The "Art of Loving:" A Road Map for the Cube of Love[*]

The following table is a list of Ignatian Ideals as expressed by a Principle followed by an example of the same concept found in the "Art of Loving."

Ignatian ideals
describe the creative and collegial habits of effective leaders.

"The Art of Loving"[†]
transcends cultures, religions, and systems of ethics.

The Principles of Good Practice[‡]
guides policy and professional practice.

---

[*] The Cube of Love is a simple, innovative way to transform individual behavior and group dynamics into harmonious reciprocal relations that foster universal brotherhood. See http://www.focolare.org/usa/professional-life/education-2/cube-of-love/

[†] James, M., Masters, T. & Uelmen, A., *Education's Highest Aim: Teaching and Learning Through a Spirituality of Communion.* 2010. New City Press: Hyde Park, NY.

[‡] Estanek, S. M. & James, M. J. (2010). *Principles of good practice for student affairs at Catholic colleges and universities: Second edition with diagnostic queries* [Brochure]. Chicago, IL: Association of Catholic Colleges and Universities, Association for Student Affairs at Catholic Colleges and Universities, Jesuit Association of Student Personnel Administrators.

Ignatian Ideal "Art of Loving"	Principles of Good Practice *Examples*
Reverence	Principle 5: Challenges students to high standards of personal behavior and responsibility through the formation of character and virtues
Love the Other as Yourself	*See the good in the nature and abilities of yourself and the other; Understand challenges, difficulties, and problems as opportunities for good; Promote the good, truth, and beauty in everyone*
Finding God in all things	Principle 1: Welcomes all students into a vibrant campus community that celebrates God's love for all
Love Everyone	*See everyone as an ally, colleague, or partner in the institutional mission; Make a conscious effort for "transparency"; Give priority to communication. Keep all "stakeholders" in the loop*
Be attentive	Principle 4: Creates opportunities for students to experience, reflect upon, and act from a commitment to justice, mercy, and compassion, and in light of Catholic social teaching to develop respect and responsibility for all, especially those most in need
Share the Other's Joy or Hurt	*Give priority to the perspective or point-of-view of the other: "Walk in the shoes" of the other. Make their perspective your own: Set aside your beliefs and ideas to understand the other*

Cura personalis	Principle 3: Enriches student integration of faith and reason...
Love Your Enemy	*Embrace difficulties and challenges as golden opportunities: Recognize your adversaries as a gift, providing special relationships and insights: Be ready to "start again"*
Creative companionship in service	Principle 6: Invites and accompanies students into the life of the Catholic Church through prayer, liturgy, sacraments and spiritual direction
Be the First To Love	*Take the initiative to help the other; Be the first to say a kind word and do a kind deed; Share constructive ideas and resources*
Men and women for others	Principle 7: Seeks dialogue among religious traditions and with contemporary culture to clarify beliefs and to foster mutual understanding in the midst of tensions and ambiguities
Love One Another	*Commit yourself to the good of your constituents, colleagues, and community; Share our hopes, ideas, needs, time, and gifts; Accept what others offer as if it were your own.*

Further Reading

Education's Highest Aim: Teaching and Learning Through a Spirituality of Communion, James, M., Masters, T., and Uelmen, A., New City Press. ISBN 978-1-56548-336-1 $14.95

Principles of good practice for student affairs at Catholic colleges and universities: Second edition, with diagnostic queries [Brochure]. Chicago, IL: Association of Catholic Colleges and Universities, Association for Student Affairs at Catholic Colleges and Universities, Jesuit Association of Student Personnel Administrators, Estanek, S. M. & James, M. J. (2010). Available for download at http://www.accunet.org/files/public/REV4PrinciplesofGoodPractice.pdf

Other Resources

The Cube of Love and *The Cube of Peace*

The Cubes are a simple, innovative way to transform individual behavior and group dynamics into harmonious reciprocal relations that foster universal brotherhood. People learn how to resolve conflicts and create a new culture based on mutual respect and concern becoming co-builders of peace.

Available at http://www.focolare.org/usa/professional-life/education-2/cube-of-love/

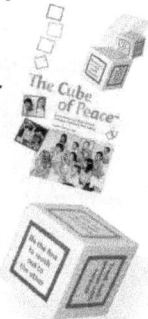

New City Press

of the Focolare

Hyde Park, New York

New City Press is one of more than 20 publishing houses sponsored by the Focolare, a movement founded by Chiara Lubich to help bring about the realization of Jesus' prayer: "That all may be one" (John 17:21). In view of that goal, New City Press publishes books and resources that enrich the lives of people and help all to strive toward the unity of the entire human family. We are a member of the Association of Catholic Publishers.

Further Reading
www.NewCityPress.com

Other Books in the 5 Step Series:

...to Facing Suffering	978-1-56548-502-0	$4.95
...to Living Christian Unity	978-1-56548-501-3	$4.95
...to Positive Political Dialogue	978-1-56548-507-5	$4.95

Scan to join our mailing list for discounts and promotions

Periodicals
Living City Magazine, www.livingcitymagazine.com

of this book. And the twin goal of "building the community" becomes, to a certain extent, both the method and the consequence of individuals who are discovering God-Love. The choices of individuals in response to their community (i.e., the relationships that come about) will either damage the community or build it. And the identity of those individuals becomes defined by these choices.

Taking the Five Steps

This student leadership development guide is made up of five chapters, each corresponding to an aspect of the "Art of Loving." The "Art of Loving" is born from an ethos of reciprocal human interaction such as in the Golden Rule. Practitioners have developed a helpful tool called the Cube of Love. Each side of a six-sided die is labeled with a component of the "Art of Loving:"

- Love the other as yourself
- Love everyone
- Share the other's joy or hurt
- Love your enemy
- Be the first to love
- Love one another

At a given moment, often at the beginning of the school day or at the beginning of a meeting, the group will roll the Cube and take the result as their watchword. At another moment, often at the end of the day or the end of an event, students and faculty or supervisors share their experiences of living that particular aspect of the "Art of Loving" throughout the day. Using the Cube of Love has helped schools, office environments, athletic teams, residence halls, and student leader organizations to establish a consistent ethos, transforming their cultures from ones based on rules to ones based on relationships. This changed way of being translates not only into interpersonal relationships, but also into extracurricular activities, student development programming, and academic performance.

Within each chapter or "Step," readers will find:

- **A point** from the "Art of Loving" followed by a concept from Ignatian spirituality

- **A compelling case** for practicing these concepts in daily life enlightened by scripture, Church documents, and student development research

- **Concrete suggestions** for putting the concept into practice. Suggestions are informed by scripture, church teaching, and one of the *Principles for Good Practice for Student Affairs at Catholic Colleges and Universities*

- **An inventory** for personal reflection on how each of us can begin to implement the practice on a deeper level
- **A "real-life story"** from students about how they have tried to put the concept into practice
- **A checklist** of actions that you might take to move towards the concepts suggested in the chapter

Step 1

Love One Another:
Men and Women for Others

Be the First to Love:
Creative Companionship

Love Your Enemy:
Cura Personalis

Share the Other's Joy or Hurt:
Be Attentive

Love Everyone:
Finding God in All Things

Love the Other as Yourself: *Reverence*

The Point

IMAGINE FOR A MOMENT that you are making your way to class and you see a student texting and walking. Completely engrossed in his or her phone screen, the student is oblivious to anything beyond that tunnel vision—other people, the sky, the weather, and surroundings. Suppose that battery dies. Instantly the student's vision expands beyond what had just been easiest and most immediately interesting to take in all those people and things that were previously being ignored.

This broadening of perception from tunnel vision to a more panoramic view of the periphery is the first step in the "Art of Loving." Once you have begun to practice loving the other as yourself (reverence), the next step is to love everyone. This is also expressed in the Ignatian ideal to *"find God in all things."*

"The Sheep and the Goats"

"Lord, when was it that we saw you hungry and gave you food, or thirsty and gave you something to drink? And when was it that we saw you a stranger and welcomed you, or naked and gave you clothing? And when was it that we saw you sick or in prison and visited you?" And the king will answer them, "Truly I tell you, just as you did it to one of the least of these who are members of my family, you did it to me."

(Mt 25:37b-40)

Why Do We "Love Everyone?"

Before we can meditate on how to practice "love everyone," we must tackle the question, "Why do we love everyone?" And the answer to that question is really simple. Because *everyone* is made in the image of God!

The Case

"Creation Story"

> Then God said, "Let us make humankind in our image, according to our likeness; and let them have dominion over the fish of the sea, and over the birds of the air, and over the cattle, and over all the wild animals of the earth, and over every creeping thing that creeps upon the earth." So God created humankind in his image, in the image of God he created them; male and female he created them.
>
> (Gn 1:26-27)

God made humankind with a special dignity not bestowed on any other living thing, and that dignity was being made in His image. This can speak to us in two important ways.

1. **Being made in the image of God means our worth and value are inherent.**

And by inherent, we mean that it is "existing" in someone or something permanently. Often, we value ourselves and others based on data in our resumes, GPAs, number of clubs joined or Facebook friends. Can you think of any others?

The one string uniting all of these criteria is that they are *external* to us, and often result from *what we do*.

To practice the "Art of Loving," we must think differently. Our dignity and value is not external, but *inherent*; not dependent on what we do, but *who we are: made in the image of God (Imago Dei)*.

Within an educational setting, we love everyone not by appreciating what they can do for us, who they can connect us to, what reference they can give, but *by loving them for who they are*.

2. Since we are made in the image of God, in God we find how we are called to live most authentically.

If God is in essence a community of self-giving love between Father, Son, and Holy Spirit *and* we are made in the image of God, *then* we live most authentically when we live in communities of self-giving love.

> The Lord Jesus, when He prayed to the Father, "that all may be one ... as we are one" (Jn 17:21-22) opened up vistas closed to human reason, for He implied a *certain likeness between the union of the divine Persons, and the unity of God's sons [and daughters] in truth and charity* [emphasis added]. This likeness reveals that man, who is the only creature on earth which God willed for itself, cannot fully find himself except through a sincere gift of himself.
>
> *Pastoral Constitution*
> *on the Church in the Modern World:*
> *Gaudium et Spes* [Joy And Hope], sec. 2

How Do We "Love Everyone?"

A Principle of Good Practice for
Student Affairs at Catholic Colleges
and Universities:

*Welcomes **all students** into a vibrant
campus community that celebrates
God's love for all.*

Student affairs professionals at Catholic colleges and universities are committed to creating
inclusive, welcoming campus environments in
which members celebrate the diversity of all in
both faith and culture. Their works, actions, and
programs reflect respect, justice, collaboration,
and dialogue.

"The Good Samaritan"

(A scholar of the law) who wished to justify himself, said to Jesus, "And who is my neighbor?" Jesus replied, "A man was going down from Jerusalem to Jericho, and fell into the hands of robbers, who stripped him, beat him, and went away, leaving him half dead. Now by chance a priest was going down that road; and when he saw him, he passed by on the other side. So likewise a Levite, when he came to the place and saw him, passed by on the other side. But a Samaritan while traveling came near him; and when he saw him, he was moved with pity. He went to him and bandaged his wounds, having poured oil and wine on them. Then he put him on his own animal, brought him to an inn, and took care of him. The next day he took out two denarii, gave them to the innkeeper, and said, 'Take care of him; and when I come back, I will repay you whatever more you spend.' Which of these three, do you think, was a neighbor to the man who fell into the hands of the robbers?" He said, "The one who showed him mercy." Jesus said to him, "Go and do likewise."

(Lk 10:29–37)

How Can *I* Love Everyone?

In a time and place where you can reflect in silence, ask yourself these questions:

- Who is in my "tunnel vision?" Who do I already find it easy to love?

- Do I believe that my dignity, being made in the image of God, is inherent?

- Do I tie my self-perception to external factors?

- What external factors mean more to me than they should?

- Who are people I normally consider "outsiders?" How can I be like the Good Samaritan toward them?

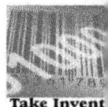

Real-Life Story
No matter how busy you are

KATIE: As student leaders, we frequently find ourselves running from class to class, meeting to meeting, and spending the "down time" in between crouched over our laptops and books in the library. In the pursuit of our fullest selves, it is sometimes easy to forget to share our love with each other. When we are this busy, how can we share this internal light with the people around us?

A wise man once advised the world to "stop and smell the roses." Including others in the aura of your internal light, no matter how busy you are, is not impossible. Each day, take a moment to reach out to a friend, colleague, or stranger and share with them your love. While there are myriad ways of doing so, my favorite is by means of conversation.

Do not underestimate the power of conversation. Even brief dialogue and thoughtfulness can transform someone's outlook on his or her day. In my college dining hall, for instance, I always take a minute or two to chat with the cashiers, even if I am grabbing a soda and rushing off to class. I venture beyond the safe conversation of "How are you," "Good, fine, thanks," and ask them about their weekend or if they have had a chance to enjoy the sunshine. Through the accumulation of these short but meaningful encounters, I have become acquainted with a wonderful woman named Marie. Although I only see Marie for a couple minutes a week, she always calls me by my first name and asks how my classes have been or if my asthma is getting any better. When I approach the counter, her face becomes alive. It lights up with the kind of love that you can share with others through just an ounce of genuine thoughtfulness.

Similarly, the other day I stopped on my way to class to chat with a janitor who was mopping the stairs in my residence hall. After a couple of minutes of small talk about our hockey team, I thanked him for his hard work and assured him that everyone in my building appreciates what he does for us. He thanked me, and never stopped smiling. His sheer joy warmed me from the inside out, and made being a couple minutes late to class one hundred percent worth it.

Conversations are key to spreading the love that you find within yourself. Whether you mentor an underclassman, help a friend through a difficult time, or strike up a conversation with a stranger in the elevator, you are spreading your love to the world. How you choose to include others in your light is up to you, but do not forget the importance of dialogue. It can be simple and brief, but even thirty seconds of thoughtfulness can leave a lasting impression on others. Take the time to smell the roses, and you will find the light inside of you and that of the world growing brighter and brighter.

- What was Katie's favorite way of practicing "love everyone?"

- What are the most meaningful conversations you've had? How can you use conversation as a way to "love everyone?"

"Love Everyone"

Checklist

❑ See everyone as an ally, colleague, or partner in the education mission.

❑ Make a conscious effort for "transparency."

❑ Give priority to communication. Keep all "stakeholders" in the loop.

❑ Say hi to someone to whom you normally might not.

❑ Invite other groups on campus to collaborate on programming.

❑ _____

❑ _____

(Add any actions you might think of, too!)

_____

_____

_____

_____

_____

_____

_____

_____

_____

_____

Step 2

The Point

*O*NCE WE HAVE OPENED our eyes and expanded our viewpoint to see the other person, we allow ourselves the opportunity to step out of our own worlds and into theirs. If we are to enter fully into that life of the other, though, we must be intentional in our efforts to pay attention to their experiences and to what might be going on beneath the surface.

Simple daily interactions are a great place to start; they often have much greater impact than we realize. Think of a time in the last week when you could have engaged in a meaningful conversation with a peer or coworker but felt you were too busy to talk for more than a few minutes. Did you ask how their weekend was and go on with your day? Did either of you gain anything from that conversation?

Often our own worries, responsibilities, and issues prevent us from knowing and understanding our neighbors; they keep us from entering into relationships that we think can't be fit into our already-packed lives or that we are scared to enter into in the first place. For example, the awkwardness of sitting next to a peer on a bus and trying to spark up conversation can feel agonizing. The practice of being attentive demands a level of discomfort that most of us would prefer to avoid, but we cannot give priority to what is happening in the life of the other if we are not paying attention.

Why Do We Share the Other's Joy or Hurt?

Being attentive gives us the opportunity to recognize and understand the perspective of the other, thus allowing us to get outside of ourselves and walk in their shoes. Walking in another's shoes involves letting go of our own strong beliefs, opinions, and ideas and making the other's perspective our own. This is difficult, and can make us vulnerable as we try to let go of our worries, failures, or imperfections. So why do this? Is it reasonable to expect that we can really incorporate this practice into our daily lives?

In the Spiritual Exercises, St. Ignatius offers some insight into why, as believers, we want to—and can—live out this attribute. As beings made in God's image, we strive to be more like our Creator. And when we are presented with the option to take a more divine perspective and actually choose that path, we become more alike and build our relationship with the one in whose image we have been made. Because God's son became one of us to share our joys

and sufferings, we are being more like Jesus when we do the same.

How Do We Share the Other's Joy or Hurt?

As involved students, how do we model an inclusive style of leadership that creates communities rather than individualistic advancement? As we compete against our peers for internships, coveted leadership positions, and institutional resources, do we understand their needs, goals, and desires? Or are we only concerned with our own personal goals?

A Principle of Good Practice for Student Affairs at Catholic Colleges and Universities:

Creates opportunities for students to experience, reflect upon, and act from a commitment to justice, mercy, and compassion, and in light of Catholic social teaching to develop respect and responsibility for all, especially those most in need

Because the framework of the Catholic social tradition is vital to the work of student affairs professionals in Catholic institutions, it is important for these professionals to become familiar with the tradition and to incorporate it into learning opportunities for students. Central to this work is deepening students' awareness of local, national, and international injustice and grounding this understanding through creative partnering with diverse, underserved communities. Ample opportunities for action and reflection will help all to grow, individually and collectively, in their knowledge and practice of this rich tradition, thereby contributing to the

"At the Home of Martha and Mary"

Now as they went on their way, he entered a certain village, where a woman named Martha welcomed him into her home. She had a sister named Mary, who sat at the Lord's feet and listened to what he was saying. But Martha was distracted by her many tasks; so she came to him and asked, "Lord, do you not care that my sister has left me to do all the work by myself? Tell her then to help me." But the Lord answered her, "Martha, Martha, you are worried and distracted by many things; there is need of only one thing. Mary has chosen the better part, which will not be taken away from her."

(Lk 10: 38-42)

27

common good and building a more humane and just world.

How Can *I* Share
the Other's Joy or Hurt?

In a time and place where you can reflect in silence, ask yourself these questions:

Take Inventory

- What struggle do I most need to overcome, or what might I need to let go of to allow myself to pay better attention to the needs and concerns of those around me?

- Where do I see God at work in my relationships with others?

- How do I let others share in my joy or hurt?

Real-Life Story

Stopping to ask a real question

KATIE: I started thinking about the shallowness of my passing conversations while at a BC dining hall.

"Hi!"

"Hey! How are you!?"

"Good, you?"

These little snippets are not disingenuous, just impatient. There isn't even enough time in the small time (within sight and earshot) for the second person to respond! And because I walk places so fast, I end up tootling around on my phone or remaking to-do lists when I could have stopped to ask the acquaintance a real question. I thought of at least five people that I've waved to for four years without ever stopping. Though understandable—we can't be close to everyone—it's a shame. Though Boston College has a reputation for being a friendly school, I couldn't help but realize how superficial some of these friendships are.

After this moment of self-reflection in the sandwich line, I turned around to find my roommate chatting with someone she knew from a summer service trip. Her lunch date, Paige, had lived on my hall—directly across—sophomore year, but we'd never exchanged more than a few words. Both trying to be polite, we started talking about shallow things. I mean, it was sad that the summer was over, and it had been quite hot the past few days, but I could have this conversation with a librarian or a new neighbor! I'd known this girl for two years! I decided to use this opportunity to delve deeper.

I knew (thanks to Facebook) that she'd been abroad for a whole year, studying in two different places. Once I'd asked her a few questions about that and shared that I, too, had just been abroad, we started talking about the strange transition we'd just been through. Returning from another country, where it's possible to be relatively anonymous and more independent takes a lot of adjustment. She started talking about her changing group of friends, and her reverse "culture-shock." We'd each been changed by our experiences in so many ways; we knew it would be difficult to come back to our "old life." It was amazing how easy it became to talk as real friends.

This conversation has helped me continue trying to share the other's joy around BC's campus. I've found out that there are few benefits to rushing through life, especially while at college. I've always admired others' willingness to care, and now I have begun to discover how easy it is to be that person.

- How did Katie enter into the life of another that day? Why might this have been difficult for Katie to do?

- Can you think of an example of a "superficial" relationship in your life? How does that relationship play out in the day-to-day? Have there been opportunities to share in their joy or hurt?

"Share the Other's Joy or Hurt"

Checklist

❑ Try to look at arguments from all perspectives and all angles.

❑ Put myself in another's shoes before making judgments about them.

❑ Pay attention to feelings that arise when talking to a friend about a problem they're having, or about an accomplishment they've had.

❑ Make an effort to go beyond the "culture of nice." Try to have a genuine, authentic conversation today.

❑ _____

❑ _____

(Add any actions you might think of, too!)

_____

_____

_____

_____

_____

_____

_____

_____

_____

Step 3

Steps

5

Love One Another:
Men and Women for Others

Be the First to Love:
Creative Companionship

Love Your Enemy:
Cura Personalis

Share the Other's Joy or Hurt:
Be Attentive

Love Everyone:
Finding God in All Things

Love the Other as Yourself: *Reverence*

The Point

IMAGINE FOR A MOMENT that you are on a ship at sea, and you find someone adrift in a lifeboat. If your ship passes close, it will be very easy to help — you will only have to let the survivor climb aboard. If the lifeboat is far away and can barely be seen, however, you will need to change your course. It will require more time and effort to maneuver close enough to rescue the survivor.

This extension of help, even to someone who is not close to us, is the next step in the "Art of Loving." Once you have begun to practice sharing the other's joy or hurt, the next step is extending this practice even to those for whom we initially feel little or no empathy or love: those we perceive as enemies. To do this, the Ignatian ideal of *cura personalis* or "care for the whole person" is helpful. It will be explained in the suggestion on page 36.

Why Do We Love Our Enemies?

Before we can meditate on how to practice "love your enemy," we must address the question, "Why do we love our enemies?" And the answer is really simple. Because Jesus, in His preaching, said to not be content with showing love only to those whom we find it easy to love! From Mt 5:43-48 Jesus states matters fairly clearly:

The Case

> "You have heard that it was said, 'You shall love your neighbor and hate your enemy.' But I say to you, Love your enemies and pray for those who persecute you, so that you may be children of your Father in heaven; for he makes his sun rise on the evil and on the good, and sends rain on the righteous and on the unrighteous. For if you love those who love you, what reward do you have? Do not even the tax collectors do the same? And if you greet only your brothers and sisters, what more are you doing than others? Do not even the Gentiles do the same? Be perfect, therefore, as your heavenly Father is perfect.

How Do We Love Our Enemies?

We can begin to "love our enemy" by suspending our pre-judgments and assumptions. To illustrate this, it is helpful to extend the shipwreck analogy from the opening of this chapter. Consider the scenario where the shipwrecked person is close to the ship already. In that instance, we see the person up close and accurately. Now consider the second scenario where the shipwrecked person is farther away. In that case, the literal distance will coincide with a mental distance — between what we imagine the person might look or be like and what is the person's true appearance and personality. As long as there is distance, there will always be that discrepancy. To love our enemies, then, we must close that gap, *suspend our pre-judgments and assumptions about the person.*

In college, we encounter students, faculty, and others from a variety of unfamiliar geographical locations, cultures, upbringings, and viewpoints . We must consider that our "enemies" — those we find annoying or otherwise disagreeable — have been formed differently than we have, and so react to situations differently.

Cura personalis is the Ignatian ideal of attending to the care and development of the "whole" person.

Creatively look for **graces *already present*** in the person or situation.

Creatively look for **graces *that are possible*** in your relationship with this person.

These two ways to "love our enemies" involve *cura personalis*. Loving our enemies requires us to resist the temptation to focus upon and magnify in others what annoys, disappoints, or repels us about their actions or personality. Succumbing to that temptation reduces others to a two-dimensional caricature of their true and authentic selves. Therefore, with a humble sense that not everything about us is fully agreeable to those we encounter, we must creatively look for graces *already present* or *possible* in others—regarding our would-be "enemy" as a whole, multi-dimensional person: *cura personalis*.

Sometimes we perceive someone as an enemy because of a particular incident in our relationship. Another key to loving our enemy is forgiveness. Hate only begets hate. Only forgiveness can break the cycle. Hate continues to harm, but forgiveness absorbs a past wrong for the sake of love and a new beginning. And our Teacher was the first to show us how, even at the hands of those who were crucifying him...

> ### "Forgiveness"
>
> Two others also, who were criminals, were led away to be put to death with him. When they came to the place that is called The Skull, they crucified Jesus there with the criminals, one on his right and one on his left. Then Jesus said, "Father, forgive them; for they do not know what they are doing." And they cast lots to divide his clothing.
>
> (Lk 23:32-34)

Student affairs professionals who work in the Catholic tradition and serve in institutions of higher learning have a twofold call: to articulate a compelling truth as we understand it and to search for an informed truth as we explore it. While the first is supported by the rich heritage and reflection of a faith community, the second entails openness to other traditions and experiences. Educational institutions thrive on dialogue respectful of differences of points of

Principle of Good Practice for Student Affairs at Catholic Colleges and Universities:

Seeks dialogue among religious traditions and with contemporary culture to clarify beliefs and to foster mutual understanding in the midst of tensions and ambiguities

view, and the consequent uncertainties and tensions are vital to the learning mission of colleges and universities. Thus student affairs professionals serving in Catholic colleges and universities honor other faith traditions and experiences and invite them into dialogue for purposes of exploration and insight.

How Can I Love My Enemy?

In a time and place where you can reflect in silence, ask yourself these questions.

Take Inventory

- Who I have I cut out of my life? Who have I walled off from myself?

- Am I willing to work a little more to close the distance between myself and someone I perceive as an enemy?

- Which perceptions of my "enemy" are true and which are assumptions that I have made or find it easier to believe than the truth?

- How can I build on graces or strengths already present in my "enemy?"

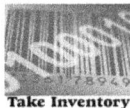

Real-Life Story
A Gift

MARIA: It was 9:00 p.m. on a Wednesday night in February, only two short weeks before Boston College's housing lottery was scheduled to begin. I was walking back to my Residence Hall after an hour-long meeting, carrying 72 pages of reading still hot from the printer. Although I was upset with myself for not starting my history homework earlier, I was fairly confident that I could have all three articles read by 12:30 a.m. Just as I was approaching my residence hall, however, my cellphone rang, potentially shattering all hope of getting to bed at a reasonable hour. It was my friend Olivia[*] calling from a study room in O'Neill Library. From the shakiness of her voice, I could tell she had been crying. "What's the matter?" I asked, nervously awaiting an explanation.

Olivia told me that she had been in the library, shut off in that study room, for almost an hour. One of her roommates, Katharine—the one she had felt closest to, in fact—had just told Olivia that none of her current roommates wanted to live with her the following year. I believe the words Katherine used were "too nice." Olivia was "*too nice*" to live with them, whatever that meant. Through frustrated words and barely audible sniffles, Olivia asked me to come to the library

---

[*] Names in this story have been changed.

and talk with her. She didn't have anywhere else to go. The last thing Olivia wanted was for people to see her crying, and she certainly wasn't going back to her room to face five girls who had just stabbed her in the back.

I had a choice to make. Either I could tell Olivia I had too much homework to do and promise to see her first thing tomorrow, ensuring I would get some much needed sleep, or I could head back to the building I had just left and be present for a friend in need. Someone once told me that there are two ways to see another person: as a gift or as a threat. Though Olivia was one of my closest friends, in this moment I unquestionably viewed her as a threat. I knew that if I were to go talk with her, I would be there for at least two hours. Either my home-work or my sleep would suffer, for I would not be able to do both well if I returned to my room at 11:00 p.m. not having started my his-tory readings.

As I was making up my mind, I recalled the ideal of "Love Your Enemy," and remembered hearing about the positive effects of embracing difficulties as golden opportunities. Now was as good a time as any to practice the attribute of courage. I decided to see Olivia as a gift, not a threat, and embraced this challenge as a chance to strengthen our friendship. I will never for-get the gratitude evident on Olivia's face when I walked into that study room with gummy bears and Oreos, ready and willing to listen. Even though I had to finish my reading in the hallway outside my bedroom door and did not get to sleep until 3:00 a.m., I knew I had made the right choice.

- How did Maria perceive Olivia at first as a threat? Why didn't she regret changing her mind?

- Who or what life situations do you perceive as threats? How might you view these as gifts or opportunities?

"Love Your Enemy"

❑ Embrace difficulties and challenges as golden opportunities.

❑ Recognize your adversaries as a gift, **Checklist** providing special relationships and insights.

❑ Be ready to "start over."

❑ Practice active listening *and* listening first, before speaking.

❑ Eliminate "enemy" from your vocabulary.

❑ Embrace difficulties and challenges as golden opportunities.

❑ _____

❑ _____

(Add any actions you might think of, too!)

_____

_____

_____

_____

_____

_____

_____

_____

Step 4

Love One Another:
Men and Women for Others

Be the First to Love:
Creative Companionship

Love Your Enemy:
Cura Personalis

Share the Other's Joy or Hurt:
Be Attentive

Love Everyone:
Finding God in All Things

Love the Other as Yourself: *Reverence*

The Point

*A*FTER BUILDING UP THE courage to love our enemies, we must act on that courage to truly live like Christ and strengthen our relationship with God. This requires using that courage to take the first step—being the first to reach out, the first to start a conversation, the first to love.

Most of us find being the first to love terrifying and risky. It requires an unfamiliar way of being social, a different equation for social interaction. It is easy to enter into a relationship with and show love to those who have given the go-ahead to interact with them. We generally have no problem showing love to a roommate, a family member, or a teammate. But what about everyone else? It's uncertain how others, especially strangers or people we don't know well, will accept our kindness and our love. We cannot wait for someone else to open the door. We must open it first.

Why Are We
the First to Love?

Ignatian spirituality calls us to look for God in every part of our life—every day, every action, and every personal encounter. We often seek God's call in our vocation. What must I do to fulfill his will—to serve him and his creation? Who is he calling me to be? Similarly, the "Art of Loving" asks us to turn to God, to be attentive to how he is present in our lives and in our daily interactions with others, to ask, *"What is the will of God in this moment, with this person?"* The answer is simple: to love that person. We are called to love. Through that love, we most fully experience the love of God.

The Case

We are constantly being filled with God's grace, God's love. But we are also called to respond to that grace and build on it by sharing it with others. Even though our pride or insecurities might make this difficult, we will become more capable of giving and receiving that grace if we practice the "Art of Loving."

Living in Community

But if by this social life the human person is greatly aided in responding to his destiny, even in its religious dimensions, it cannot be denied that men are often diverted from doing good and spurred toward and by the social circumstances in which they live and are immersed from their birth. To be sure the disturbances which so frequently occur in the social order result in part from the natural tensions of economic, political and social forms. But at a deeper level they flow from man's pride and selfishness, which contaminate even the social sphere. When

> the structure of affairs is flawed by
> the consequences of sin, man, already
> born with a bent toward evil, finds there
> new inducements to sin, which cannot be
> overcome without strenuous efforts and the
> assistance of grace.
>
> *Pastoral Constitution on the
> Church in the Modern World:
> Gaudium et Spes* [Joy And Hope], sec. 25.

How Can We Be the First to Love?

How do we take initiative, to be the first to say a kind word or do a good deed? The first step is recognizing that everyone is worthy of your love. Whether it is a stranger or someone who has treated you poorly, each deserves your love because like you, they are made in the image of God.

It is also important to be the first to respond positively. While in a meeting or working on a group project for example, responding negatively can stifle the group's creativity and energy. But being attentive to the good intentions of those around us allows us to share constructive ideas and resources, thus using the best ideas and talents in the room for the success of the entire group.

Finally, when practicing being the first to love, we must also pay attention to those courageous folks who are the first to love us. When another reaches out, we must be willing to accept that love. This can be hard to do, and it is also easy to miss if we have made prior assumptions about others' intentions.

Principles of Good Practice for
Student Affairs at Catholic Colleges
and Universities:

Invites and accompanies students into the life of the Catholic Church through prayer, liturgy, sacraments and spiritual direction

Catholic colleges and universities assist all students to develop an active and meaningful relationship with God. This is accomplished through such activities as traditional and contemporary prayer opportunities, small faith sharing groups, retreats, spiritual direction, and (upon request) RCIA [Rite of Christian Initiation for Adults] instruction. In addition, liturgical and sacramental opportunities are scheduled on a regular basis for Catholic students. Each student's personal relationship with God can be further deepened by application of the charisms and spiritual practices of the institution's founding religious order, where applicable.

In many Catholic institutions the campus ministry staff is part of the student affairs division. In other Catholic institutions student affairs professionals collaborate with members of the campus ministry staff. In welcoming students to the salvific richness of Jesus Christ, student affairs professionals have a responsibility to understand and articulate the Catholic faith and to support and work with campus ministers to provide pastoral care and leadership to students seeking spiritual growth.

How Can *I* Be The First To Love?

In a time and place where you can reflect in silence, ask yourself these questions.

- How has my own self-doubt crippled my ability to love?

- What can I do to slow down so that I recognize the opportunities God gives me to step out and be the first to show love?

- When has someone shown love to me? How did it make me feel?

- How does being the first to love strengthen our relationship with God?

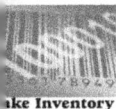

Real-Life Story
Men and women
for and with others

KENNY: After an incredible birthday week-end in New York City, I boarded a bus back to Boston College. I got lucky with an awesome seat on the bus at a table with some very comfortable legroom. There were still three vacant seats around the table and our bus was relatively empty as we departed. About two hours into the trip we got word that another bus from the same company had broken down on its way to Boston from Washington, DC and that ours was going to take on some of its passengers. A mother, a third-grade boy, and his twenty-year-old brother from Tennessee all sat at the table with me. I decided to take my headphones out and start a conversation with them. I quickly learned that while I just had one of the best weekends of my life, they were having the worst. They left Tennessee at six that morning and had already been traveling for close to eighteen hours when they boarded my bus. Their bus from Washington, DC was stuck on the side of the road for two hours and the family already missed their 10:15 p.m. connection from Boston's South Station to their final destination Bangor, Maine. They got lucky and were able to schedule an 11:15 p.m. bus from South Station to Maine, which would still be another four-hour trip. This however was all before the mother said to me that none of them had eaten since they left Tennessee at 6:00 a.m.

I talked with them throughout the two hours we had left until we reached Boston. While I had been dreading just traveling from New York City for four hours I realized that this family was going through something I could not imagine. I learned that they were going to a family reunion to meet the mother's new nephew and to visit her father's grave. I played card game after card game with the two boys and shared some great laughs along the way. I told them about all of the sights in Boston and a little bit of my story as a student at Boston College and growing up in New England. Those two hours flew by in no time. We arrived at South Station and the family had to rush right to their next bus. Getting off, I was not ready to say goodbye yet because I was so full of their love but at the same time I had so much empathy for their situation. These people had gone twenty hours without a single bite of food. So I decided I needed to put my love into action and help this family during the worst day of their summer. I got off and immediately ran to McDonald's around the corner in the terminal. I bought four number 2 meals with four Sprites, one for me and three for them. It was 11:12 p.m. when I got the food and I chaotically sprinted down the middle of South Station and finally found them still in line just about to board. When they saw me coming they all looked very confused but when I handed the mother the food, she was in shock. A tear ran from her eye and the boys' eyes widened like it was Christmas morning. It was pure joy on their faces. I will never forget that look as long as I live.

The mother all of a sudden realized she did not yet know my name. She asked me and after I told her she thanked me, gave me a big hug, and I wished them farewell. As I walked away the boy yelled back to me with his southern hospitality, "God bless you!" It was right then that I knew God was present. He put me on that bus to help that family. I was meant to be sitting at that table where nobody chose to sit at first. Boston College's motto, "Men and women for and with others" rang in my heart so powerfully that night that I left South Station and boarded the T back to BC with the biggest smile I have ever had on my face.

It was on the train back that I decided to check Facebook on my phone and I suddenly had a new friend request. It was the mother. She had remembered my name. I immediately accepted the request and this time a small tear fell from my eye. I was the first to love but she was attentive and loved me right back. She and her family left Maine later that week and she posted a status: "Leave Maine tonight and heading to D.C. This was a wonderfully relaxing trip that brought me lots of laughter, tears, and new memories. God has been so good to me." I read that one morning when I woke up and again was reminded of how God is ever present in the world. The most honest thing I have ever known is that God is love and his love is everlasting because he works through people. I was the first to love not by being a hero or saving a life, but by simply buying a hungry family some food.

- How was Kenny the first to love? Did this take courage?

- What apprehensions might Kenny have had on his trip that would have kept him from loving these strangers?

"Be the First to Love"

❑ Remember that everyone is worthy of love.

❑ Challenge the status quo for social interaction on campus.

Checklist

❑ Make the effort to understand the other's perspective before making assumptions about their intentions.

❑ Look for moments today where God is calling you to love.

❑ _____

❑ _____

(Add any actions you might think of, too!)

_____

_____

_____

_____

_____

_____

_____

_____

_____

_____

Step 5

Love One Another:
Men and Women for Others

Be the First to Love:
Creative Companionship

Love Your Enemy:
Cura Personalis

Share the Other's Joy or Hurt:
Be Attentive

Love Everyone:
Finding God in All Things

Love the Other as Yourself: *Reverence*

The Point

IMAGINE FOR A MOMENT that you are a professional musician, a violinist perhaps. You have the score for an orchestral arrangement, and you are seated alone onstage in a full concert hall. Surely when you play the part for the violin, you will play it well. And for one violinist, it could not possibly sound any better or fuller. However, within the larger context of an orchestra, with the expertise of other musicians, their scores, and their instruments, there is a possibility of something more, and something fuller— *but it cannot be realized alone. It can only be realized with others.*

Such collaboration is the next step in the "Art of Loving." Once you have begun to practice being the first to love, the next step is collaboration, being able to "harmonize" our gifts and personalities with the gifts, talents, needs, and personalities of others in a spirit of reciprocity.

Why Do We Love One Another?

The Case

The answer to that question is really simple: We love one another because we are *called to love as Jesus loved us*. John 13:34-25 makes it clear:

I give you a new commandment, that you love one another. Just as I have loved you,

you also should love one another. By this everyone will know that you are my disciples, if you have love for one another."

In fact, the roots of the "Art of Loving" can be traced to Chiara Lubich, a teacher in Italy who, during World War II, came to embrace a certain passage in the Bible. We also love one another because we are *called to be united as one human family as God is united within the Trinity.*

"Unity, Chiara Lubich, and Focolare"

As they took refuge from the bombings in a dark cellar, they opened the gospel and read by candlelight the solemn page of Jesus' prayer before dying: "I ask not only on behalf of these, but also on behalf of those who will believe in me through their word, that they may all be one. As you, Father, are in me and I am in you, may they also be in us, so that the world may believe that you have sent me" (Jn 17:20–21).... As Lubich remembered, "*One thing was clear in our hearts: what God wanted for us was unity. We live for the sole aim of being one with him, one with each other, and one with everyone. This marvelous vocation linked us to heaven and immersed us in the one human family. What purpose in life could be greater?*" [emphasis added] (*Essential Writings* 17).

Michael James et al., *Education's Highest Aim* (Hyde Park NY: New City Press, 2010), 35.

How Do We Love One Another?

We love one another by being more aware of our own gifts and potential, as well as those of others. The onus does not lie entirely on us to do everything ourselves, although the pace of contemporary society and collegiate life may make it seem like we are living in a jungle where everyone has to fend for himself or herself. Instead, by loving one another, appealing to others' gifts when we need help or stepping up when others need us, we help build community and collaboration that enables us to do much more together than any of us ever could have done alone.

The Ignatian ideal of "men and women for others" is key to our understanding of *how* we love one another. We are not men and women in isolation, but men and women interconnected, interdependent, and in community. To become "men and women for others" involves:

- being *attentive* to those around us, those we readily see and those we do not, as well as to those in need and their needs, and to the ways in which we are all connected;

- being *reflective* about others' needs, our abilities, others' talents, and our own;

- being *active* by translating our reflection into reality, "harmonizing" our gifts and talents with the diverse gifts and talents

of others to work towards answering
the calls of those in need in our society...
in other words, being *contemplatives in
action*!

Principle of Good Practice for Student Affairs at Catholic Colleges and Universities:

*Enriches student integration of faith
and reason through the provision of
co-curricular learning opportunities*

The Catholic tradition has always valued and
engaged in dialogue about the interconnection
and integration of faith and reason. This dialogue
and integration is a legitimate and significant
part of Catholic higher education. Catholic colleges and universities foster the development of
the whole person. In addition to rigorous intellectual development, there is particular emphasis on a student's faith and spiritual development.
In collaboration with academic colleagues, student affairs professionals provide educational
opportunities and learning experiences outside
the classroom that complement learning in the
classroom, such as living-learning residential
communities, volunteer service activities, and
service-learning opportunities. Catholic colleges and universities provide opportunities for
students to develop a habit of reflection and to

value prayer in bringing both faith and reason to the discernment process of how to live out their learning experiences and the values of Catholic higher education in their personal and professional lives. Catholic colleges and universities also provide opportunities for intellectually informed and robust conversations on important issues of faith and culture, including applying relevant Catholic teaching to these issues.

"Golden Apple"

The golden apple of selfhood, thrown among the false gods, became an apple of discord because they scrambled for it. They did not know the first rule of the holy game, which is that every player must by all means touch the ball and then immediately pass it on. To be found with it in your hands is a fault: to cling to it, death. But when it flies to and fro among the players too swift for eye to follow and the great master Himself leads the revelry, giving Himself eternally to His creatures in the generation, and back to Himself in the sacrifice, of the Word, then indeed the eternal dance "makes heaven drowsy with the harmony."

C.S. Lewis, *The Problem of Pain*
(New York: Harper Collins, 1940), 158

How Can I Practice
"Loving One Another?"

In a time and place where you can reflect silently, ask yourself these questions.

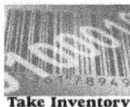

Take Inventory

- What are my gifts and talents? Where are my weaknesses?

- How can I "harmonize" my gifts with gifts of other people in my dorm? Class? Clubs?

- What are the pressing needs on my campus? Where are the opportunities for unity?

- When in the past have I practiced reciprocity? Where have I seen good examples of collaboration?

Real-Life Story
Being in community
with those around you

TEDDY: On a Thursday in early Spring, I had meaningful experiences of mutual love at my daily meals. Paying for my egg sandwich and orange juice at the dining hall, I began to talk with Ada, the cashier, about each of our families and how we each celebrate the Easter season. We both laughed about how our families eat so much on Easter brunch. We then high-fived before I went off to my first class.

My dinner was shared with a few little boys who were at a temporary psychological and behavioral unit where I volunteer. For an hour I had them explain to me how to play different card games and the rules of football, even though I knew everything that they were telling me. However, they took such pride in sharing what they knew with me, that I kept pretending that I had no idea.

None of these conversations may seem like anything out of the ordinary, but they really do define what it means to be in community with those around you. I was very different than the people with whom I shared these moments. We had different ages, races, sexes, faiths, socioeconomic backgrounds, and jobs. However, each one was vitally important for my day. "Being men and women for others" does not have to mean starting a non-profit or donating all of your clothes to the poor. It can be seen as being men and women *with* others. The high five, the intent listening, and the courteous curiosity were all examples of just being there for someone else in my life. Striving to give the best version of myself to others every day is not only very fulfilling, but it benefits each and every person I come in contact with. And in this giving of myself I gain the gifts of receiving insights about an appreciation for and the necessity of the other in my life.

- How did Teddy practice "love one another?" Does practicing "love one another" always involve large and grand deeds?

"Love One Another"

Checklist

☐ Commit yourself to the good of your constituents, colleagues, and community.

☐ Share our hopes, ideas, needs, time, and gifts.

☐ Accept what others offer as if it were your own

☐ Be attentive to the gifts and needs of others.

☐ Build community by practicing and sharing the six attributes of the "Art of Loving."

☐ _____

☐ _____

(Add any actions you might think of, too!)

_____

_____

_____

_____

_____

_____

Appendix

Student Leadership and The "Art of Loving:" A Road Map for the Cube of Love[*]

The following table is a list of Ignatian Ideals as expressed by a Principle followed by an example of the same concept found in the "Art of Loving."

Ignatian ideals
   describe the creative and collegial habits of effective leaders.

"The Art of Loving"[†]
   transcends cultures, religions, and systems of ethics.

The Principles of Good Practice[‡]
   guides policy and professional practice.

---

[*] The Cube of Love is a simple, innovative way to transform individual behavior and group dynamics into harmonious reciprocal relations that foster universal brotherhood. See http://www.focolare.org/usa/professional-life/education-2/cube-of-love/

[†] James, M., Masters, T. & Uelmen, A., *Education's Highest Aim: Teaching and Learning Through a Spirituality of Communion*. 2010. New City Press: Hyde Park, NY.

[‡] Estanek, S. M. & James, M. J. (2010). *Principles of good practice for student affairs at Catholic colleges and universities: Second edition with diagnostic queries* [Brochure]. Chicago, IL: Association of Catholic Colleges and Universities, Association for Student Affairs at Catholic Colleges and Universities, Jesuit Association of Student Personnel Administrators.

Principles of Good Practice
Examples

Ignatian Ideal "Art of Loving"	Principles of Good Practice *Examples*
Reverence	Principle 5: Challenges students to high standards of personal behavior and responsibility through the formation of character and virtues
Love the Other as Yourself	*See the good in the nature and abilities of yourself and the other; Understand challenges, difficulties, and problems as opportunities for good; Promote the good, truth, and beauty in everyone*
Finding God in all things	Principle 1: Welcomes all students into a vibrant campus community that celebrates God's love for all
Love Everyone	*See everyone as an ally, colleague, or partner in the institutional mission; Make a conscious effort for "transparency"; Give priority to communication. Keep all "stakeholders" in the loop*
Be attentive	Principle 4: Creates opportunities for students to experience, reflect upon, and act from a commitment to justice, mercy, and compassion, and in light of Catholic social teaching to develop respect and responsibility for all, especially those most in need
Share the Other's Joy or Hurt	*Give priority to the perspective or point-of-view of the other: "Walk in the shoes" of the other. Make their perspective your own: Set aside your beliefs and ideas to understand the other*

Cura personalis	Principle 3: Enriches student integration of faith and reason…
Love Your Enemy	*Embrace difficulties and challenges as golden opportunities: Recognize your adversaries as a gift, providing special relationships and insights: Be ready to "start again"*
Creative companionship in service	Principle 6: Invites and accompanies students into the life of the Catholic Church through prayer, liturgy, sacraments and spiritual direction
Be the First To Love	*Take the initiative to help the other; Be the first to say a kind word and do a kind deed; Share constructive ideas and resources*
Men and women for others	Principle 7: Seeks dialogue among religious traditions and with contemporary culture to clarify beliefs and to foster mutual understanding in the midst of tensions and ambiguities
Love One Another	*Commit yourself to the good of your constituents, colleagues, and community; Share our hopes, ideas, needs, time, and gifts; Accept what others offer as if it were your own.*

Further Reading

Education's Highest Aim: Teaching and Learning Through a Spirituality of Communion, James, M., Masters, T., and Uelmen, A., New City Press. ISBN 978-1-56548-336-1 $14.95

Principles of good practice for student affairs at Catholic colleges and universities: Second edition, with diagnostic queries [Brochure]. Chicago, IL: Association of Catholic Colleges and Universities, Association for Student Affairs at Catholic Colleges and Universities, Jesuit Association of Student Personnel Administrators, Estanek, S. M. & James, M. J. (2010). Available for download at http://www.accunet.org/files/public/REV4PrinciplesofGoodPractice.pdf

Other Resources

The Cube of Love and *The Cube of Peace*

The Cubes are a simple, innovative way to transform individual behavior and group dynamics into harmonious reciprocal relations that foster universal brotherhood. People learn how to resolve conflicts and create a new culture based on mutual respect and concern becoming co-builders of peace.

Available at http://www.focolare.org/usa/professional-life/education-2/cube-of-love/

New City Press
of the Focolare
Hyde Park, New York

New City Press is one of more than 20 publishing houses sponsored by the Focolare, a movement founded by Chiara Lubich to help bring about the realization of Jesus' prayer: "That all may be one" (John 17:21). In view of that goal, New City Press publishes books and resources that enrich the lives of people and help all to strive toward the unity of the entire human family. We are a member of the Association of Catholic Publishers.

Further Reading
www.NewCityPress.com

Other Books in the 5 Step Series:

...to Facing Suffering	978-1-56548-502-0	$4.95
...to Living Christian Unity	978-1-56548-501-3	$4.95
...to Positive Political Dialogue	978-1-56548-507-5	$4.95

Scan to join our mailing list for discounts and promotions

Periodicals
Living City Magazine, www.livingcitymagazine.com